Governo
Readi

A Grand Canyon
Journey *Tracing Time in Stone*

by
Peter Anderson

A First Book

FRANKLIN WATTS   *A Division of Grolier Publishing*
New York • London • Hong Kong • Sydney • Danbury, Connecticut

ARIZONA

UTAH
COLORADO

NEVADA

GRAND CANYON
NATIONAL PARK

CALIF.

Colorado River

ARIZONA

NEW MEXICO

PACIFIC OCEAN

MEXICO

Kanab
Platea

GRAND CANYO

Lake Mead

Shivwits
Plateau

Colorado River

Coconino Plate

Colorado River

Photographs ©: Andre Potochnik: 18, 29, 49, 53 inset; Audrey Gibson: 8, 9; Ben Klaffke: 17, 32; Dennis Flaherty: 13; Folio, Inc.: 1 (Robert Rathe); Gary Ladd: cover, 20, 25, 26, 28, 35, 43, 52, 53; Larry Ulrich: 6, 15, 37, 46, 54, 55; Photo Researchers: 40 (John Cancalosi/OKAPIA), 47 (Will/Deni Mcintyre); Superstock, Inc.: 10, 11 (John W. Warden), 21; Tom Bean: 23, 31, 33, 39.

Map (p. 2-3) and diagram (p. 56) by Joe Lemmonier.

Library of Congress Cataloging-in-Publication Data

Anderson, Peter. 1956–
    A Grand Canyon journey : tracing time in stone / by Peter Anderson.
        p. cm. — (A First book)
    Includes bibliographical references (p.) and index.
    Summary: Describes the geology, evolution, and beauty of the Grand Canyon by leading the reader down the Bright Angel Trail.
    ISBN 0-531-20259-3 (lib. bdg.)   0-516-15839-X (pbk.)
    1. Grand Canyon (Ariz.)—Description and travel—Juvenile literature. 2. Grand Canyon (Ariz.)—Geology—Juvenile literature. 3. Natural History—Arizona—Grand Canyon—Juvenile literature. [1. Grand Canyon (Ariz.) 2. Natural History—Arizona—Grand Canyon.] I. Title. II. Series.
    F788.A535 1997
    917.91'32—dc20   96-36144
                                                                                    CIP
                                                                                     AC

CONTENTS

Chapter One
Walking Through a Rainbow   7

Chapter Two
Pages of Stone   12

Chapter Three
Restless Rock   16

Chapter Four
Ancient Mud   22

Chapter Five
Tall Tales   27

Chapter Six
We Were Here   30

Chapter Seven
A Hole in Time   42

Chapter Eight
The Wonders of Water   48

Glossary   57
For Further Reading   59
Internet Resources   60
Index   61

Chapter One

Walking Through a Rainbow

To look into the Grand Canyon is to look into a rainbow of stone. As our gaze drifts down the rock layers that make up the canyon walls, colors change from tan to gold to rose to gray-green to brown to black. Below our stone rainbow runs the Colorado River, a shiny blue-green ribbon swirling through sunlight and shadow as it carves ever deeper into some of the oldest rocks in North America.

A walk into this rainbow of stone is a walk into the earth's past. The deeper we go, the older the rock layers become. Imagine yourself standing at the top of the South Rim of the canyon. The rocks here were formed 250 million years go. By the time we reach the river at the bottom of our rainbow, we will be walking on rocks that are 1.7 billion years old.

Our trek begins at the top of the Bright Angel Trail. Listen to the raven's call echoing off the cliffs below us. As the raven flies, the canyon is about 10 miles (16 km) wide right here. In other sections of the canyon, it is as much as 18 miles (28.8 km) from rim to rim. To trace the

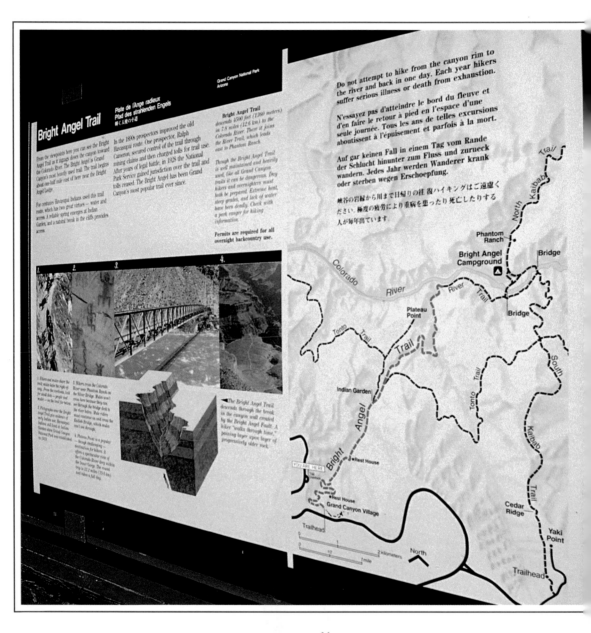

Bright Angel Trail

Piste de l'Ange radieux
Pfad des strahlenden Engels
輝く天使の小道

From the viewpoints here you can see the Bright Angel Trail as it zigzags down the canyon toward the Colorado River. The Bright Angel is Grand Canyon's most heavily used trail. The trail begins about one-half mile east of here near the Bright Angel Lodge.

For centuries Havasupai Indians used this trail route, which has two great virtues — water and access. A reliable spring emerges at Indian Garden, and a natural break in the cliffs provides access.

In the 1800s prospectors improved the old Havasupai route. One prospector, Ralph Cameron, secured control of the trail through mining claims and then charged tolls for trail use. After years of legal battle, in 1928 the National Park Service gained jurisdiction over the trail and tolls ceased. The Bright Angel has been Grand Canyon's most popular trail ever since.

Bright Angel Trail descends 4500 feet (1360 meters) in 7.8 miles (12.6 km) to the Colorado River. There it joins the River Trail, which leads east to Phantom Ranch.

Though the Bright Angel Trail is well maintained and heavily used, like all Grand Canyon trails it can be dangerous. Day hikers and overnighters must both be prepared. Extreme heat, steep grades, and lack of water have been deadly. Check with a park ranger for hiking information.

Permits are required for all overnight backcountry use.

Do not attempt to hike from the canyon rim to the river and back in one day. Each year hikers suffer serious illness or death from exhaustion.

N'essayez pas d'atteindre le bord du fleuve et d'en faire le retour à pied en l'espace d'une seule journée. Tous les ans de telles excursions aboutissent à l'épuisement et parfois à la mort.

Auf gar keinen Fall in einem Tag vom Rande der Schlucht hinunter zum Fluss und zurueck wandern. Jedes Jahr werden Wanderer krank oder sterben wegen Erschoepfung.

峡谷の岩棚から川まで日帰りの挂復ハイキングはご遠慮ください。極度の疲労により重病を患ったり死亡したりする人が毎年出ています。

8

path of the Colorado River through the Grand Canyon, a raven would have to fly more than two hundred miles.

When you and I reach the bottom of the canyon, we will be a mile closer to the center of the earth. As we descend, we will notice a rise in the temperature. In this desert climate, where a raindrop can dry up and disappear between the rim and the river, vegetation is sparse.

Below the rim, the Bright Angel Trail zigs and zags. It tunnels through rock, cuts under overhanging canyon walls, and swings around stone *buttresses*. In places, the trail is barely wide enough to accommodate the mule trains that carry visitors to the bottom of the canyon each day. Sometimes one side of the trail hugs the canyon wall while the other edges up to a sheer cliff that drops off hundreds of feet.

With each step down the trail, dust whirls out from underneath our boots and hovers for a moment before the wind carries it away. In such a dry climate, the body loses moisture rapidly. Drink a lot of water.

A mule train climbs Bright Angel Trail.

Chapter Two

Pages of Stone

Here, at the top of the trail, we stand beside a layer of buff-colored rock called Kaibab Limestone. As dry as it is, it's hard to believe that these rocks were formed underwater, 250 million years ago. Look carefully at the canyon wall beside the trail. Run your fingers across the lines and bumps you see in the limestone. These are pieces of bone and shell that are the remains of creatures who lived in an ancient sea. Remnants like these are called fossils.

Fossils are pictures left on pages of stone. They help tell the earth's life story. Sometimes they consist of animal tracks or burrows, or maybe the imprint of an insect wing or a plant leaf, that were once made in sand or mud and later hardened into rock. Sometimes they are hard body parts like shells, bones, or teeth that have been covered over and preserved in the rock layers. Shark's teeth have been found in the Kaibab Limestone. More commonly seen are petrified pieces of sponges, corals, and sea urchins, as well as mollusks such as snails and clams. All of these remnants were left behind by an ancient sea about 250 million years ago.

This Kaibab Limestone (in the foreground) is the top layer of the Grand Canyon. See page 56 for a diagram of all the rock layers.

As you ran your hand across this wall of limestone, did you notice that it was kind of gritty? That graininess means that the rock contains sand. Sand deposits suggest a shoreline environment. If we were to head east, we would find more sand in this limestone. Less gritty textures are found to the west where the limestone formed from deepwater layers of sludge.

Geologists have noticed that the fossils also change from east to west. If we followed the Kaibab Limestone to the east, we would be more likely to see shallow water species like clams and snails. If we traced this layer to the west, we would find higher numbers of deepwater species like corals. Since this ancient sea seems to have been deeper toward the west, geologists believe it came from that direction.

As you look at these fossils, imagine the waves washing over a shoreline. Wade out into the water and feel the shells of snails and clams as your toes dig into the wet sand. Now imagine yourself swimming through a warm and shallow lagoon. You dive under the water and swim past a sponge, steering clear of a sea urchin whose spines are as sharp as porcupine quills. Now picture yourself floating along the surface of a deep, clear sea. Below you a shark glides over the coral canyons that cover the ocean bottom.

Had we been able to stand in this spot for the time

it took to deposit the Kaibab Limestone, we might have seen all of these marine environments. We would have seen the water getting deeper as the ocean moved in. We would have seen the deep waters turn shallow as the same sea receded. As these marine environments changed, so did the animal populations. That's why we find both deepwater and shallow-water fossils in these canyon walls today. But why did this ancient sea come and go?

View from the South Rim

Chapter Three

Restless Rock

As solid as the surface of the earth may seem, it is constantly changing. Partly that's because the surface of our planet is composed of different pieces, or plates, that move around on a lavalike fluid called magma. As our continents float across the globe on various plates, they occasionally collide, pushing up mountain ranges like the Himalayas in Asia. Sometimes magma surges up from below, stretching a plate so taut that it tears apart. If you look at a globe and compare the coastlines of Africa and South America, you can see how they were once joined together. As the earth's plates move, continents change shape. So do our oceans and seas.

And so do rock layers like the ones we are walking through in the Grand Canyon. As continental plates collide and break up, rocks fold, crack, and fracture. If you look back up the trail you may notice that there is a natural break in the cliff walls. The gap that made a route for our trail was caused by such a fracture, called a fault. Where rocks crack, water runs. Where water runs, rocks erode. We'll talk more about this process of *erosion* later on.

Below the Kaibab Limestone and another layer of limestone called the Toroweap Formation, these canyon walls take on a yellow hue. Feel this rock and you will find that it is even grittier than the limestone above us. Notice the curved lines that swirl through the surface of this stone. These lines outline layers of sand that were deposited by the wind about 270 million years ago. It has since solidified into rock called Coconino Sandstone.

As we look into this wall of Coconino Sandstone, we are looking into the cross-section of ancient sand dunes. Lizards and scorpions once crawled across these

Coconino Sandstone (top) and Hermit Shale (bottom)

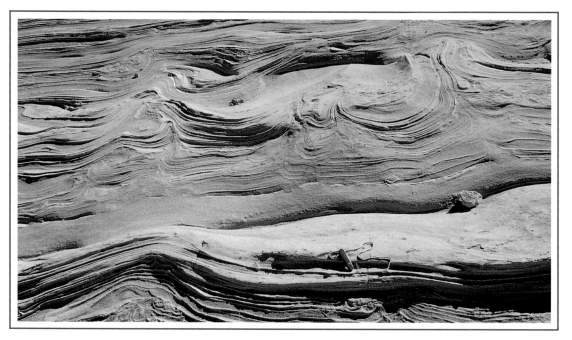

The swirling sands of ancient dunes leave their mark in this sandstone.

dunes that were as high as 300 feet (90 m) in places. How was it that this desert turned to stone?

To find the answer, we look to the wind and the sand. As the wind blows, a grain of sand bounces across a dune. The friction of each bounce grinds away rough edges. Gradually, the sand grain becomes smaller and rounder. The wind not only shapes each particle of sand, it also sorts them out because it carries lighter sand grains farther than heavy ones. These smooth, round, and sorted sand grains make an especially dense pile as they settle on top of one another.

Additional layers of sand cover them and compress them even more. Millions of years later, along comes the sea. As water filters down into the sand, it carries minerals that cement the grains together.

The stronger the bond between the minerals of a rock layer, the less it will erode. Mineral cement makes the Coconino Sandstone strong. Interlocking mineral grains do the same for the Kaibab Limestone. The Hermit Shale, which we are about to enter, has neither the cement nor the interlocking crystals to bond its minerals together. Water seeps into the resulting cracks and spaces. As the water freezes and thaws, it expands and contracts, prying loose pieces of shale that break off and begin to slide downhill.

As we descend into the red beds of the Hermit Shale, we notice places where this weak and crumbly rock layer has eroded underneath the more resistant sandstone above it. The overhanging slabs of Coconino Sandstone will eventually collapse. Occasionally someone gets to witness such an event, but we probably won't. Rocks do things on rock time. And the rock clock moves slower than ours does. In fact, if we were to come back in a thousand years or so, we would notice little, if any, change in these canyon walls.

Still, as our trail snakes through some of the tall, rose-colored *buttes* that we admired from the South Rim,

19

This canyon wall consists of the top four layers of the Grand Canyon (top to bottom): Kaibab Limestone, the Toroweap Formation, Coconino Sandstone, and Hermit Shale. The crumbly shale layer slopes much more than the limestone and sandstone layers.

it is good to remember that in rock time, these are only temporary landmarks. As permanent as they may seem to us, these monuments of stone are constantly eroding. The chisels of water and wind will gradually wear them down. Water and gravity will sweep the resulting rubble down to the river. And the Colorado River, like a never-ending freight train, will carry it all away.

The Colorado River constantly carries pieces of the canyon away.

Chapter Four

Ancient Mud

If limestone suggests sea, and sandstone suggests desert, shale says mud. The shale we are now walking on was deposited as mud in the *floodplain* and *delta* of a river that flowed through this area about 280 million years ago.

Suppose we were to travel down to the Gulf of California where the Colorado River empties into the ocean. There we would find its delta, a huge deposit of *silt* and mud, some of which eroded out of the Grand Canyon. Two hundred eighty million years ago, when the area that has become the Grand Canyon was on the edge of the sea, the sluggish rivers and streams that flowed through this region deposited similar layers of mud in floodplains, lagoons, and deltas. Like the mud layers we would find at the Colorado River delta today, these deposits contained remnants of plant and animal life.

Imagine yourself walking along the banks of a slow and muddy river. A dragonfly flits by, riding a warm breeze, and lands on the lacy leaf of a riverside fern.

You leave the shade of a riverside pine tree and walk through dried mud beds left behind by a previous flood. The sun is hot, much to the delight of some lizard-like reptiles who crawl across these cracked mudflats.

Fossilized plants, along with the beautifully preserved impression of an insect wing almost four inches long, suggest that the Hermit Shale was deposited in an environment like this. If we look at pieces of shale near the meeting place of the Hermit Shale and Coconino Sandstone, we may notice mud cracks. We might even

The Hermit Shale preserves a fossil of an ancient insect wing. Remnants such as this one help confirm that the shale was deposited in a muddy, riverside environment.

find the imprint of a 280 million year-old raindrop. For these features to have been preserved, it must have been dry, and getting dryer, when this mud hardened into stone. Eventually, this region became a desert, and the sand dunes that formed the Coconino above us covered the hardened mud of the Hermit Shale.

Looking back up at the meeting place of the Hermit and Coconino layers, we can see how different they are—the sandstone cliffs are solid and sheer, while the shale slopes are weak and crumbly. We might guess that they were deposited in very different environments, but what about the next rock layer below us? It's not as easy to tell where the Hermit Shale ends and the Supai Formation begins.

Like the Hermit Shale, the rock layers that make up the Supai Formation contain a lot of hardened mud. We can see from a quick glance down the trail that sheer cliff layers seem to alternate with crumbly slope layers. From what we have learned so far, we might guess that this formation is made up of a combination of rock layers—harder sandstones and limestones as well as softer shales. Such a guess would be correct. But what kind of environment would have produced these differing rock layers?

How about a river delta? Maybe a shallow sea? Or was it a seaside coast? The answer is all of the above.

The alternating cliff and slope layers of the Supai Formation indicate that it was deposited during a variety of conditions.

The topmost layers were deposited in a river environment—maybe that's why it's hard to tell where the Hermit ends and the Supai begins. Lower layers of the Supai were laid down as a shallow sea came and went.

25

By the time we have walked through all 950 feet (290 m) of this rock formation, this ancient sea will have come and gone at least four different times.

As that ancient sea fades into the horizon one last time, we approach our first resting place. Off to the side of the trail, we find a hut built from blocks of stone taken out of these Supai layers. Congratulations. You've made it to "Three-Mile House." We're about halfway to the bottom.

Three-Mile House on Bright Angel Trail provides welcome rest to hikers. Switchbacks leading from the shelter wind deeper into the canyon.

Chapter Five
Tall Tales

As we rest our feet and snack on a couple of apples, we see a mule train approaching. "Now, ya see those white patches down there in that next layer of stone," says a *wrangler* to the tourists riding behind him, "that's petrified snow." Our gaze drifts down to the cliffs below us. We see light grey streaks on the red cliffs. You say you've never heard of petrified snow? That's because there is no such thing. But it makes a good tale for this wrangler to tell these folks as he guides them down the trail.

Look again at the red cliffs pointed out by the wrangler. Even though we know this rock layer as the Redwall Limestone, those cliffs weren't originally red. They are made of light grey stone stained red from the water that flows down out of the Hermit and Supai layers. Sometimes, after especially heavy rains, cascades of water laden with sand pour over these cliffs. These sandy waterfalls scrape away that red coating, leaving behind those light grey patches of "petrified snow."

And here's another tale to ponder as we begin our trek down the steep *switchbacks* known as Jacob's

27

The Redwall Limestone (middle) is stained red from the Supai Formation above it. Light grey patches remain where the stained surface has been scraped away.

Ladder. Consider that these cliffs of Redwall Limestone are composed of billions of shells and skeletons left behind by billions of tiny marine organisms who lived and died in a huge ocean that covered this area 335 million years ago. How many generations of tiny creatures would it have taken to build these cliffs, some of which are almost 500 feet (150 m) high? Enough to make this rock layer the biggest graveyard you or I have ever seen.

Although the majority of the creatures that lived in this ancient sea were tiny, if not microscopic, there were other creatures, such as corals, whose remains we may see in this rock layer. Sometimes you can find the tube-like shells in which these corals spent their lives, straining tiny bits of food out of sea water. Sounds like a rough way to make a living, doesn't it?

Although limestone consists mostly of the shells and skeletons of microscopic marine creatures, the fossils of larger creatures, such as this coral, can be found in the Redwall Limestone.

Chapter Six

We Were Here

We swing across the last of the switchbacks, drop down two additional layers of limestone known as the Temple Butte and Muav limestones, and follow the trail out onto the sagebrush-covered flats known as the Tonto Platform. Here, we have left the last of the limestone cliffs behind to enter a more horizontal layer called the Bright Angel Shale. If you're used to being around a lot of green grass, the desert vegetation here—mostly sagebrush, yucca, and cactus—may seem a little stark. But compared to the world as it looked 540 million years ago when the Bright Angel Shale was deposited, this region is lush. Back then, there weren't any plants or animals living on dry land.

All of this is especially hard to imagine as we near a canopy of trees that casts an island of shade over an *oasis* known as Indian Garden. Much of the water that seeps down through the rock layers above us surfaces here in the form of springs. Garden Creek gathers up these spring waters and carries them across this shelf of shale. Around these waters grow grasses and grapevines and berries and thick, leafy cottonwood

The thick canopy of trees over Indian Garden stands out from the sparse surrounding vegetation.

Prickly pear cactuses flourish in Indian Garden.

trees. Such an oasis in the midst of these gray-green hills probably caught the attention of the hunters who once roamed this territory.

Our knowledge of these early hunters began with a discovery made in 1933. Several workers who had been building a trail in the depths of the canyon decided to take time out for some exploring. On the floor of a cave a few miles from here, they found four-legged animal figures that had been made from pieces of a plant called split willow. *Archaeologists* believe that

This split willow figure is about four thousand years old.

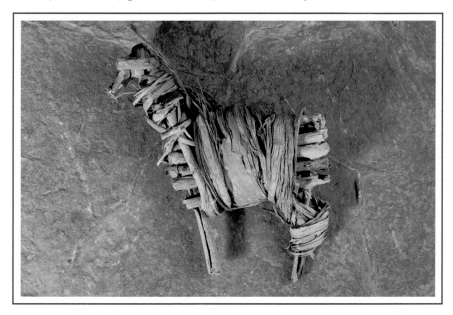

these figures were meant to represent the deer or bighorn sheep that still roam the *benches* of the Tonto Platform. Twigs that pierce the forelegs of these animal figures suggested spears. Scientists using radio-carbon dating techniques have determined that these figures are about four thousand years old.

Not too far from here, tucked away in cliffs of sandstone, are the remains of dwellings left behind by native people known to us as the Anasazi or "ancient ones." Here in Indian Garden, and elsewhere in the Grand Canyon, they grew corn, beans, and squash and utilized various native plants. All around the Tonto Platform grows a spiky plant that sometimes shoots up a tall, spindly stalk. It is called yucca, and the Anasazi put it to good use. They made sandals, rope, and baskets from its fibers. With its roots, they produced a kind of soap. Archaeologists have found fire pits in which the edible parts of the yucca were roasted.

Sometime during the late 1200s, the Anasazi left their canyon dwellings, probably because of a severe *drought*. That left a vacancy for a tribe of hunter-gatherers, known as the Cerbats, who moved into this region about 150 years later. Descendants of these people include the Havasupai, or "people of the blue-green water." The Havasupai take their name from the turquoise waters that flow by their home on Havasu

The Anasazi Indians left the canyon long ago, but their dwellings remain.

Creek, which enters the Grand Canyon from the south. These Indian people grew crops and lived seasonally at Indian Garden well into the 1800s.

    The Havasupai have their own stories about the Grand Canyon. They speak of two gods, Tochopa and Hokomata, who once quarreled. Hokomata threatened to drown the world. Tochopa built a boat for his daughter, Pukeheh, to protect her in the event of a flood.

Tochopa was wise to have done so, because Hokomata soon lived up to his threat. First, a great rumbling was heard. Then a wall of water roared like a thousand rivers across the land. But inside the log boat her father had built for her, Pukeheh rode out the great flood. As the flood began to recede, the waters rushed like a great tide toward the sea, carving a deep *chasm* in the earth. It was here that Pukeheh's boat finally came to rest.

Like a butterfly leaving a cocoon, she emerged from her boat and entered the world. It was a dark world emptied of people. They had all been swept away in the great flood. Here at the bottom of this deep chasm, she wondered if she would ever find a husband.

Then Pukeheh noticed a light in the eastern sky. The rising sun brought hope. Eventually, it brought Pukeheh her first child. And as the sun had fathered her first child, a waterfall fathered the second. So it was that the "people of the blue-green water" came to live in the bottom of the Grand Canyon.

While the Havasupai are the only Indian people who still live in the depths of the Grand Canyon, other Indian nations—the Hualapai, Kaibab-Paiute, Hopi, and Navajo—live nearby. Some of their stories also speak

The Havasupai Indians derive their name from the blue-green waters of Havasu Falls.

of great floods in the distant past. The Hualapai, for instance, tell of a giant called Packithaawi, who was able to swim in the rising floodwaters. He stuck his knife in the earth, pounded it down with his war club, and cut a deep gash. When the floodwaters drained out to the sea, the Grand Canyon was revealed.

As we walk across the Bright Angel Shale, traces of sea creatures that lived in this region 540 million years ago remind us of the stories that geologists tell of an ancient ocean. We can learn from the fossil record that the ocean waters that came and went during this particular period were teeming with life.

On dry land, the world was empty and silent—not a single sign of life. Out in the shallow waters, however, it was different. There were shellfish and seaworms. Jellyfish bobbed on gentle waves. Crab-like trilobites crawled through the ooze on the seafloor.

Close your eyes, and let the world go dark for a moment. Imagine yourself underwater. Maybe you feel the tug of the tides. Perhaps you notice changes in the ocean temperature. Prior to the evolution of eyesight, the experience of primitive sea creatures was limited to these kinds of sensations.

During this era, when the Bright Angel Shale was deposited, the trilobite may have been the first creature on earth to see the world it lived in. Although the

These Hualapai Indian children live near the Grand Canyon.

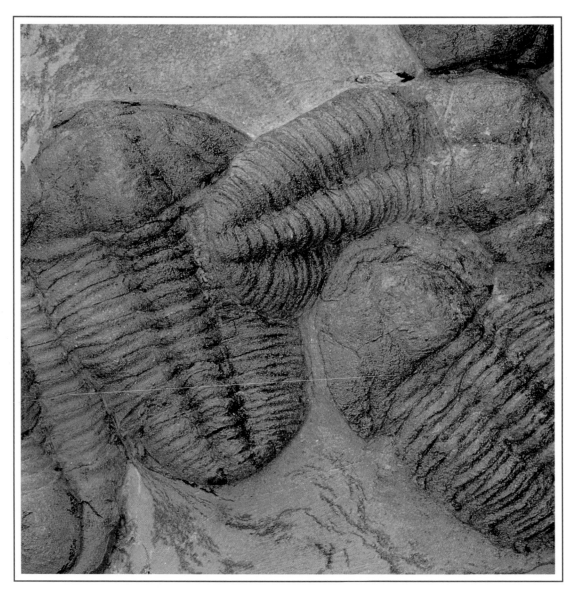

Fossils such as these are all that remain of the trilobites.

largest trilobites found in the Grand Canyon are only a little more than three inches long, they have been known to reach lengths of two feet or more. A close-up look at a trilobite fossil suggests a bug-like creature—maybe a miniature horseshoe crab. Like crabs, trilobites had the defensive advantage of owning a shell. Despite any resemblance to modern-day creatures, the trilobites left no living relatives.

Nevertheless, they remind us of their presence. "We were here," say fossilized tracks in the shale, left by a wandering trilobite 540 million years ago. Look back up at the Kaibab Limestone. Right about the time that the Kaibab was beginning to form, the trilobites disappeared from the scene. By the time they disappeared, the trilobites had survived as a species for more than 200 million years. No other creature, not even the dinosaur, has enjoyed as long a stay on planet earth.

Whether or not we humans will be as successful remains to be seen. We may not be able to see very far into the future, but at least you and I can travel back in time as we trek into this rainbow of stone. From the Kaibab Limestone to the Bright Angel Shale, we have covered more than 300 million years in a distance of about 5 miles (8 km). That averages out to about twenty thousand years for each step you have taken.

41

Chapter Seven

A Hole in Time

Soon we enter the Tapeats Narrows, a deep *cleft* carved out of a sandstone layer that looks a little like piecrust. As we come to the end of this piecrust layer, we are poised on the brink of a deep hole in time. The step that takes us out of the Tapeats Sandstone and into the dark and twisted rock layer below it carries us across a canyon of time that is 1.2 billion years wide. In one step, we will cross more than four times the amount of earth history that we have covered in the 5 miles (8 km) between here and the rim. What's going on?

Suppose we could make a movie out of the earth's life story. Since the earth, according to most scientists, is about 4.6 billion years old, this might be a very long movie. Let's say it would take a year to see the whole film.

In this, the world's longest movie, the oldest rocks in the Grand Canyon, which have been here for 1.7 billion years, wouldn't appear until the end of August. The Tapeats Sandstone would appear in November. Trilobites would star from mid-November until sometime in early December. The Kaibab Limestone would

About 1.2 billion years of rock is missing between the Tapeats Sandstone (top) and the Vishnu Schist (bottom). Accordingly, this junction is called the Great Unconformity.

appear several hours later. Dinosaurs would be featured for about a week and a half beginning in mid-December. Mammals would appear during the final week. And our earliest humanoid ancestors would show up at about 5 a.m. on the last day of the year. Human beings, as we know them, would arrive just in time to see the very end of the film and celebrate the new year.

As we walk farther into the canyon, it is as if we are watching a portion of this movie run backwards. When we reach the edge of the Tapeats Sandstone, where we are now standing, the screen goes blank and stays that way for almost three months. There should be 1.2 billion years worth of rock layers between the Tapeats Sandstone, which is about 550 million years old, and the Vishnu Schist, which is about 1.7 billion years old, making it the Grand Canyon's oldest rock layer. If it's true, as geologists say, that these missing layers were once 12,000 feet (3,658 m) thick, what happened to all that rock?

Erosion. That's what. To fully grasp the impact of erosion on our rainbow of stone, let's begin with the dark and tilted rock below us that we call the Vishnu Schist. More than two billion years ago, hardened lavas along with a thick sequence of rock layers, not unlike the ones we have been walking through today, covered this region. Movement of the earth's plates folded and buried these layers, which were then cooked by heat from the earth's core. Collisions of the earth's plates caused these "cooked" rocks to reemerge in the form of mountains about 1.7 billion years ago.

One thousand feet (300 m) of Vishnu Schist, the dark rock layer between here and the river, is all that remains of a mountain range that would have towered 15,000 to 20,000 feet (4,500 to 6,000 m) over our heads. Imagine these phantom mountains—higher than the Rockies—rising up into the sky.

How do mountains like these disappear? The process begins with rain. As it rains, water seeps through cracks and joints in the stone. Chemicals in the water dissolve small grains of rock. Later on, the water freezes and thaws, prying loose bigger pieces of rock. These rocks grind against other rocks as they slide downhill. The wind carries away particles of dust left behind by these grinding rocks. In the end it can be said that wind, water, and gravity have hauled away these mountains, but that's only part of our erosion story.

After these ancient mountains were worn down to their roots, new layers of rock were deposited. Then wind and water went to work again, grinding away another 12,000 feet (3,658 m) of rock layers. In some areas, like the area where you and I happen to be standing, these rock layers were entirely worn away.

About 1,000 feet (300 m) of this Vishnu Schist is the only trace of a mountain range that once towered almost 20,000 feet (6,000 m) high.

In other parts of the Grand Canyon, many of these rock layers remain. That's one way that geologists know what is missing here in front of us. It may seem unbelievable, but water, wind, and gravity carried off all this stone.

The silt-laden waters of the Colorado River (right) contrast with the relatively clear waters of the Little Colorado River (left). The clouds of sediment remind us that these rocks are constantly eroding away.

Chapter Eight
The Wonders of Water

You hear a rumbling sound. Here, where the trail winds through the Tapeats Narrows, the dark canyon walls press in close, leaving only a narrow slit of sky above our heads. It almost feels as if this dark gorge is about to swallow us up.

As we near the end of the Narrows, we are relieved to see sunlight pouring into these dark shadows from a widening patch of sky up ahead. Soon the walls of the Narrows flare out on either side of us. We find ourselves standing on a rock ledge about 100 feet (30 m) above the source of that deep, rumbling sound: the Colorado River.

Here in the desert, we are naturally drawn to water. We wouldn't last long here without it. We are struck by the swirling currents in the sparkling river and the bright white waves of distant rapids. It's as if the river is tugging at us as our path loops down through the dark schist, back and forth, back and forth, curving one way and then another. As we near the bottom of the Devil's Corkscrew, we notice the fragrance of the river—something like the scent of a fresh rain.

The Tapeats Narrows

Weary as we are, we keep moving, knowing that cool water works wonders on hot, tired feet. After we dip our bare feet in a shallow pool, we follow a riverside trail upstream, walking in between the black rock cliffs of the inner gorge that tower 1,000 feet (300 m) above us. Soon we find ourselves standing on a bridge that spans the Colorado River.

In the swirling waters below us, we notice murky clouds of *sediment* floating by. Even water this slow and smooth carries tiny particles of the canyon away. On rainy days, this green water churns brown with additional sediment that washes in from side canyons. Each piece of the canyon that moves downstream—from the tiniest particle to the biggest boulder that rolls over in the riverbed—adds to the cutting action that has carved this mile-deep (1.6-km-deep) chasm.

The river is both a freight train, hauling away the eroded debris that once belonged to these canyon walls, and a saw, whose blade is made of sand and stone. On an average day, the river carries 80,000 pounds (36,287 kg) of sediment past this bridge where we are now standing. Since it began carving the Grand Canyon, the river has removed more than 1,000 cubic miles (approximately 4,170 cu km) of sediment.

Yet, as we look from the river back up toward the rim, it is hard to imagine that a river, only a couple of hundred feet across, could have carved out a canyon that is 18 miles (28.8 km) wide in places. For good reason. The river only cut a narrow swath through this rainbow of stone. Its *tributaries* did the rest.

Sometimes the action is fast and furious. On December 4 and 5, 1966, 14 inches (36 cm) of rain pelted the North Rim of the canyon in less than 36 hours. Cascades gushed over canyon walls. Sheets of water rushed across rocky canyon soils. Streams poured into side canyons, such as Crystal and Bright Angel, and surged into 40-foot (12-m) walls of foaming mud and water, ripping out trees like weeds. Car-sized boulders cracked into each other as the great tide carried them down to the river.

Although *flashfloods* often follow heavy rains in the canyon, they usually aren't as powerful as the floods of '66. Often, the waters that widen the canyon arrive in a less forceful way. As snows melt in the spring, and storms roll through during the rainy months, trickles pour into streams, that pour into creeks, that eventually pour into the river. As they make their way to the river, each carries a piece of the canyon away. These tributaries, more than the river itself, have widened the canyon. Eventually, they will probably grind the canyon down to a broad valley. But that won't happen any time soon. Remember, we're talking rock time.

Sudden downpours such as the one in the distance can lead to ferocious flash floods (inset).

And while we're talking rock time, let's talk about the canyon itself. How long has it been here? You may be surprised to learn that the time it took for the river to carve the Grand Canyon is only a tick or two of the rock clock's second hand. Of course, a tick or two on the rock clock means millions of years—in this case about six million. That's still plenty of time for a river to get a lot of carving done.

And as a river carves out rock, it can change its own channel, and curve off in new directions. So geologists aren't sure what the Colorado River looked like long ago, or even where it flowed exactly. They just know that the river has been here long enough to carve this rainbow of stone we call the Grand Canyon, and for this they are grateful. When it comes to earth history, geologists like a good story. And there are stories that only this canyon can tell.

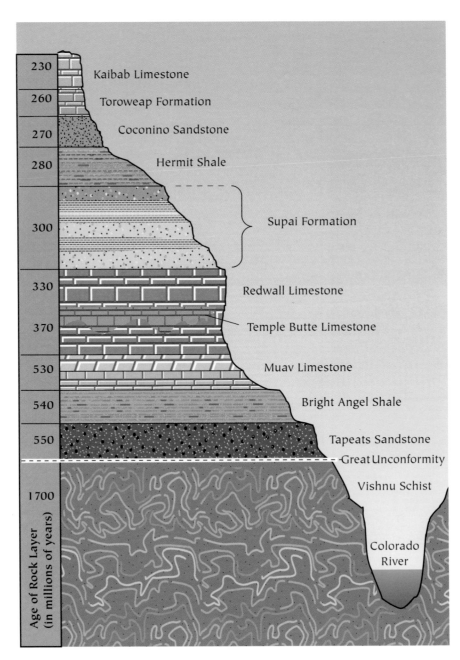

Age of Rock Layer (in millions of years)	
230	Kaibab Limestone
260	Toroweap Formation
270	Coconino Sandstone
280	Hermit Shale
300	Supai Formation
330	Redwall Limestone
370	Temple Butte Limestone
530	Muav Limestone
540	Bright Angel Shale
550	Tapeats Sandstone
	Great Unconformity
1 700	Vishnu Schist
	Colorado River

A diagram of the layers of the Grand Canyon.

GLOSSARY

Archaeologist: a scientist who unearths the remains of ancient cultures in order to learn about the human past.

Bench: a flat earth shelf.

Butte: a narrow and isolated rock formation with steep sides and flat top.

Buttress: a towerlike rock formation.

Chasm: a deep canyon; a wide crack in the earth's surface.

Cleft: a crack or crevice.

Delta: a large triangular deposit of silt and mud at the mouth of a river.

Drought: a lack of rain.

Erosion: the process of wind and water wearing away soil and rock.

Flashflood: a sudden destructive flood, often in a predominantly dry environment.

Floodplain: a low-lying area often flooded by a neighboring river.

Geologist: a scientist who studies the structure of rock layers that reveal the earth's history.

Oasis: an isolated, well-watered area in the middle of a desert.

Sediment: particles of matter carried and then deposited by wind or water.

Silt: fine sand, clay, or soil carried by moving water.

Switchback: a part of a trail that zigs and zags down a steep slope.

Tributary: a stream or river that flows into a larger river or lake.

Wrangler: a cowboy.

FOR FURTHER READING

Fraser, Mary Ann. *In Search of the Grand Canyon.* New York: H. Holt and Co., 1995.

Rawlins, Carol. *The Grand Canyon.* Austin, Tex.: Raintree Steck-Vaughn, 1995.

Young, Donald. *The Sierra Club Book of Our National Parks.* Boston: Little, Brown, 1990.

INTERNET RESOURCES

Because of the changeable nature of the Internet, sites appear and disappear very quickly. These resources offered useful information on the Grand Canyon at the time of publication. Internet addresses must be entered with capital and lowercase letters exactly as they appear.

Yahoo
http://www.yahoo.com/

The Yahoo directory of the World Wide Web is an excellent place to find Internet sites on any topic.

Grand Canyon Official Tourism Page
http://www.thecanyon.com/

This site dedicated to the Grand Canyon is sanctioned by the National Parks Service. It offers much information about the canyon and explains how to obtain perimits for various hikes in the canyon.

The "Unofficial" Grand Canyon National Park Home Page
http://www.kaibab.com/

This comprehensive guide to the Grand Canyon is run by a knowledgeable canyon enthusiast. It contains sections on canyon history, weather, maps, and lodging, to name a few. The site also features an archive of images of the canyon.

INDEX

Italicized page numbers indicate illustrations.

Anasazi, 34, *35*
Archaeologists, 33, 34

Bighorn sheep, 34
Bright Angel Canyon, 51
Bright Angel Shale, 30, 38–41
Bright Angel Trail, 7, 9, *19–11*, 16, 19, 26, *26*, 30, 48
Buttes, 19, 30
Buttresses, 9

Cactuses, 30, *32*
Cerbat Indians, 34
Coconino Sandstone, 17, *17*, 19, *20*, 23, 24
Colorado River, 7, 9, 20, *21*, 22, 45, 47, 48, 50–51, 55

Continental plates, 16, 44–45
Cottonwood trees, 30–33
Crystal Canyon, 51

Deer, 34
Deltas, 22
Devil's Corkscrew, 48
Dinosaurs, 41, 44
Drought, 34

Erosion, 16, 19, 20, 22, 44–47, 50–51, 55

Flashfloods, 51, *53*
Floodplains, 22
Fossils, 12, 14, 23, *23*, *29*, 38, *40*, 41

Garden Creek, 30
Geologists, 14, 38, 47, 55

Great Unconformity,
  the, *43*
Gulf of California, 22

Havasu Creek, 34
Havasu Falls, *37*
Havasupai Indians,
  34–36
Hermit Shale, *17*, 19, *20*,
  23–24, *23*, 25, 27
Hokomata (Havasupai
  god), 35–36
Hopi Indians, 36
Hualapai Indians, 36,
  38, *39*

Indian Garden, 30, *31*,
  32, 35

Jacob's Ladder, 27–29

Kaibab Limestone,
  12–15, *13*, 17, 19,
  20, 41, 42
Kaibab-Paiute Indians,
  36

Limestone, 12–15, *13*, 17,
  19, *20*, 22, 27–29,
  28, *29*, 30, 41, 42

Magma, 16
Mineral cement, 19
Muav Limestone, 30
Mud, 12, 22–26, 38

Native Americans,
  33–38
Navajo Indians, 36
North Rim, 51

Oceans, ancient,
  12–15, 19, 24,
  25–26, 29, 38

Packithaawi, 38
Pukeheh, 36

Radio-carbon dating
  techniques, 34
Ravens, 7
Redwall Limestone,
  27–29, *28*, *29*

Sagebrush, 30
Sand, 12, 14, 17,
    18–19, *18*, 24
Sand dunes, 17–19, *17*, 24
Sandstone, 17–19, *17*,
    18, 22, 23, 24,
    42–44, *43*
Sediment. *See* Silt
Shale, *17*, 19, *20*, 22–24,
    23, 27, 30, 38–41
Silt, 22, *47*, 50–51
Sludge, 13
South Rim, 7, *15*, 19
Split willow, 33
Split willow figures,
    33–34, *33*
Supai Formation,
    24–26, *25*, 27, *28*
Switchbacks, 27, 30

Tapeats Narrows, 42,
    48, *49*

Tapeats Sandstone,
    42–44, *43*
Temple Butte
    Limestone, 30
"Three-Mile House,"
    26, *26*
Tochopa (Havasupai
    god), 35–36
Tonto Platform, 30, 34
Toroweap Formation,
    17, *20*
Trilobites, 38–41, *40*,
    42

Vishnu Schist, *43*,
    44–45, *46*

Wranglers, 27

Yucca, 30, 34

ABOUT THE AUTHOR

Peter Anderson has worked as a river guide, carpenter, newspaper reporter, writing teacher, editor, and wilderness ranger. He has written a dozen books for young readers on topics related to nature, American Indians, and the history of the American West.